Come to M

"Come to my house,"
said the spider.

2

"No, thank you,"
said the beetle.

"Come to my house," said the spider.

4

"No, thank you,"
said the fly.

"Please, please, come to my house," said the spider.

"No, thank you,"
said the moth.

"I will come to your house," the bird said.

"No, thank you," said the spider.